The
Evolution of English Lexicography

by

James A.H. Murray

The Evolution of English Lexicography
by James A.H. Murray

ISBN: 978-93-61428-65-4

Published by

DOUBLE 9 BOOKS

2/13-B, Ansari Road
Daryaganj, New Delhi – 110002
info@double9books.com
www.double9books.com
Tel. 011-40042856

ABOUT THE AUTHOR

James A. H. Murray was a Scottish lexicographer and philologist best known for his landmark works on "The evolution of English lexicography." Murray dedicated his life to the study of language and the creation of the Oxford English Dictionary (OED), a monumental accomplishment that transformed the field of lexicography. Murray's magnum opus, "The Evolution of English Lexicography," examines the evolution of English dictionaries from their early beginnings to the cutting-edge reference volumes of the nineteenth century. Murray's landmark work examines the growth of lexicography as a topic, stressing the contributions of key personalities and technical advancements that shaped the history of English dictionaries. Murray provides insights into the challenging conditions and accomplishments of lexicographers throughout history, offering light on the intricacies of assembling and defining the English language. His work no longer just provides a comprehensive survey of lexicography, but also demonstrates the ongoing necessity of linguistic studies in preserving the richness of the English language. Murray's commitment to lexicography and seminal contributions to the discipline continue to inspire language academics and enthusiasts, establishing his legacy as a pioneer in the examination of English language and lexicography.

CONTENTS

The Evolution of English Lexicography

When the 'Act to facilitate the provision of Allotments for the Labouring Classes' was before the House of Commons in 1887, a well-known member for a northern constituency asked the Minister who had charge of the measure for a definition of the term *allotment*, which occurred so often in the Bill. The Minister somewhat brusquely told his interrogator to 'look in the Dictionary,' at which there was, according to the newspapers, 'a laugh.' The member warmly protested that, being called upon to consider a measure dealing with things therein called 'Allotments', a term not known to English Law, nor explained in the Bill itself, he had a right to ask for a definition. But the only answer he received was 'Johnson's Dictionary! Johnson's Dictionary!' at which, according to the newspapers, the House gave 'another laugh,' and the interrogator subsided. The real humour of the situation, which was unfortunately lost upon the House of Commons, was, that as agricultural allotments had not been thought of in the days of Dr. Johnson, no explanation of the term in this use is to be found in Johnson's Dictionary; as, however, this happened to be unknown, alike to the questioner and to the House, the former missed a chance of 'scoring' brilliantly, and the House the chance of a third laugh, this time at the expense of the Minister. But the replies of the latter are typical of the notions of a large number of persons, who habitually speak of 'the Dictionary,' just as they do of 'the Bible,' or 'the Prayer-book,' or 'the Psalms'; and who, if pressed as to the authorship of these works, would certainly say that 'the Psalms' were composed by David, and 'the Dictionary' by Dr. Johnson.

I have met persons of intelligence who supposed that if Dr. Johnson was not the sole author of 'the Dictionary'—a notion which, in view of the 'pushfulness' wherewith, in recent times, Dictionaries, American and other, have been pressed upon public notice, is now not so easily tenable—he was, at least, the 'original author,' from whose capacious brain that work first emanated. Whereas, in truth, Dr. Johnson had been preceded by scores of workers, each of whom had added his stone or stones to the lexicographic cairn, which had already risen to goodly proportions when Johnson made to it his own splendid contribution.

For, the English Dictionary, like the English Constitution, is the creation of no one man, and of no one age; it is a growth that has slowly developed itself adown the ages. Its beginnings lie far back in times almost prehistoric. And these beginnings themselves, although the English Dictionary of to-day is lineally developed from them, were neither Dictionaries, nor even English. As to their language, they were in the first place and principally Latin: as to their substance, they consisted, in large part at least, of *glosses*. They were Latin, because at the time to which we refer, the seventh and eighth centuries of our era, Latin was in Western Europe the only language of books, the learning of Latin the portal to all learning. And they were *glosses* in this wise: the possessor of a Latin book, or the member of a religious community which were the fortunate possessors of half-a-dozen books, in his ordinary reading of this literature, here and there came across a difficult word which lay outside the familiar Latin vocabulary. When he had ascertained the meaning of this, he often, as a help to his own memory, and a friendly service to those who might handle the book after him, wrote the meaning over the word in the original text, in a smaller hand, sometimes in easier Latin, sometimes, if he knew no Latin equivalent, in a word of his own vernacular. Such an explanatory word written over a word of the text is a *gloss*. Nearly all the Latin MSS. of religious or practical treatises, that have come down to us from the Middle Ages, contain examples of such glosses, sometimes few, sometimes many. It may naturally be supposed that this glossing of MSS. began in Celtic and Teutonic, rather than in Romanic lands. In the latter, the old Latin was not yet so dead, nor the vulgar idioms that were growing out of it, as yet so distinct from it, as to render the glossing of the one by the other needful. The relation of Latin to, say, the Romanic of Provence, was like that of literary English to Lancashire or Somerset dialect; no one thinks of glossing a literary English book by Somersetshire word-forms; for, if he can read at all, it is the literary English that he does read. So if the monk of Burgundy or Provence could read at all, it was the Book-Latin that he could and did read. But, to the Teuton or the Celt, Latin was an entirely foreign tongue, the meaning of whose words he could not guess by any likeness to his own; by him Latin had been acquired by slow and painful labour, and to him the gloss was an important aid. To the modern philologist, Teutonic or Celtic, these glosses are very precious; they have preserved for us a large number of Old English, Old Irish, Old German words that occur nowhere else, and which, but for the work of the old glossators, would have been lost for ever. No inconsiderable portion of the oldest English vocabulary has been recovered entirely from these interlinear glosses; and we may anticipate important additions to that vocabulary when Professor Napier gives us the volume in which he has been gathering up all the unpublished glosses that yet remain in MSS.

In process of time it occurred to some industrious reader that it would be a useful exercise of his industry, to collect out of all the manuscripts to which he had access, all the glosses that they contained, and combine them in a list. In this compact form they could be learned by heart, thus extending the vocabulary at his command, and making him independent of the interlinear glosses, and they could also be used in the school-teaching of pupils and neophytes, so as sensibly to enlarge their stock of Latin words and phrases. A collection of glosses, thus copied out and thrown together into a single list, constituted a *Glossarium* or *Glossary*; it was the remote precursor of the seventeenth-century 'Table Alphabetical,' or 'Expositor of Hard Words.'

Such was one of the fountain-heads of English lexicography; the other is to be found in the fact that in those distant days, as in our own, the learning of Latin was the acquisition of a foreign tongue which involved the learning of a grammar and of a vocabulary. Both grammar and vocables were probably in the main communicated by oral teaching, by the living voice of the master, and were handed down by oral tradition from generation to generation. The stock of vocables was acquired by committing to memory classified lists of words; lists of names of parts of the body, lists of the names of domestic animals, of wild beasts, of fishes, of trees, of heavenly bodies, of geographical features, of names of relationship and kindred, of ranks and orders of men, of names of trades, of tools, of arms, of articles of clothing, of church furniture, of diseases, of virtues and vices, and so on. Such lists of vocables, with their meaning in the vulgar tongue, were also at times committed to paper or parchment leaves, and a collection of these constituted a *Vocabularium* or *Vocabulary*.

In their practical use the Vocabulary and the Glossary fulfilled similar offices; and so they were often combined; the possessor of a Vocabulary enlarged it by the addition of a Glossary, which he or some one before him had copied out and collected from the glossed manuscripts of his bibliotheca. He extended it by copying into it vocabularies and glossaries borrowed from other scholars; he lent his own collection to be similarly copied by others. Several such collections exist formed far back in Old English times, the composite character of which, partly glossary, partly vocabulary, reveals itself upon even a cursory examination.

As these manuscript lists came to be copied and re-copied, it was seen that their usefulness would be increased by putting the words and phrases into alphabetical order, whereby a particular word could be more readily found than by looking for it in a promiscuous list of some hundreds or thousands of words. The first step was to bring together all the words having the same first letter. The copyist instead of transcribing the glossary right on as it stood, extracted first all the words beginning with A; then he went through it again picking out all the words beginning with B; then a third time for those with C, and so on with D, E, and the rest, till he had transcribed the whole, and his copy was no longer in the fortuitous disorder of the original, but in what we call *first-letter* order.

A still later scribe making a copy of this vocabulary, or possibly combining two or three lists already in first-letter order, carried the alphabetical arrangement one stage further; instead of transcribing the A-words as they stood, he went through them, picking out first those that began with *Aa-*, then those in *Ab-*, then those in *Ac-*, and so on, to *Az*. Then he did the same with the B-words, picking out first all in *Ba-*, then *Be-*, *Bi-*, *Bl-*, *Bo-*, *Br-*, *Bu-*, *By-*; and so exhausting the B-words. Thus, at length, in this second recension, the Vocabulary stood, not yet completely alphabetical, but alphabetized as far as the second letter of each word.

All these stages can actually be seen in four of the most ancient glossaries of English origin that have come down to us, known respectively, from the libraries to which they now belong, as the Leiden, the Epinal, the Erfurt, and the Corpus (the last at Corpus Christi College, Cambridge). The Leiden Glossary represents the earliest stage of such a work, being really, in the main, a collection of smaller glossaries, or rather sets of glosses, each set entered under the name of the treatise from which it was extracted, the words in each being left in the order in which they happened to come in the treatise or work, without any further arrangement, alphabetical or other. It appears also to incorporate in a final section some small earlier vocabularies or lists of names of animals and other classes of things. In order to discover whether any particular word occurs in this glossary, the whole work from beginning to end must be looked through. The first advance upon this is seen in the Epinal Glossary, which uses part at least of the materials of the Leiden, incorporating with them many others. This glossary has advanced to *first-letter* order: all the A-words come together, followed by all the B-words, and so on to Z, but there is no further arrangement under the individual letters[1]. There are nearly fourteen columns of words beginning with A, containing each about forty entries; the whole of these 550 entries must be looked through to see if a given word occurs in this glossary. The third stage is represented by the Corpus Glossary, which contains the materials of its predecessors, and a great deal more, and in which the alphabetical arrangement has been carried as far as the second letter of each word: thus the first ninety-five words explained begin with *Ab-*, and the next seventy-eight with *Ac-*, and so on, but the alphabetization goes no further [2] ; the glossary is in *second-letter* order. In at least one glossary of the tenth century, contained in a MS. of the British Museum (Harl. 3376), the alphabetical arrangement has been carried as far as the third letter, beyond which point it does not appear to have advanced.

The MS. of the Corpus Glossary dates to the early part of the eighth century; the Epinal and Erfurt—although the MS. copies that have come down to us are not older, or not so old—must from their nature go back as glossaries to a still earlier date, and the Leiden to an earlier still; so that we carry back these beginnings of lexicography in England to a time somewhere between 600 and 700 A.D., and probably to an age not long posterior to the introduction of Christianity in the south of England at the end of the sixth century. Many more vocabularies were compiled between these early dates and the eleventh century; and it is noteworthy that those ancient glossaries and vocabularies not only became fuller and more orderly as time advanced, but they also became more *English*. For, as I have already mentioned, the primary purpose of the glosses was to explain difficult *Latin* words; this was done at first, whenever possible, by easier Latin words; apparently, only when none such were known, was the explanation given in the vernacular, in Old English. In the Epinal Glossary the English words are thus relatively few. In the first page they number thirty out of 117, and in some pages they do not amount to half that number. In the Corpus Glossary they have become proportionally more numerous; and in the glossaries that follow, the Latin explanations are more and more eliminated and replaced by English ones, until the vocabularies of the tenth and eleventh centuries, whether arranged alphabetically or under classified headings, are truly Latin-English: every Latin word given is explained by an English one; and we see clearly that a new aim had gradually evolved itself; the object was no longer to explain difficult Latin words, but to give the English equivalents of as many words as possible, and thus practically to provide a Latin Dictionary for the use of Englishmen [3] .

Learning and literature, science and art, had attained to fair proportions in England, and in the Old English tongue, when their progress was arrested by the Norman Conquest. The Norman Conquest brought to England law and organization, and welded the country into a political unity; but it overthrew Old English learning and literary culture. In literary culture the Normans were about as far behind the people whom they conquered as the Romans were when they made themselves masters of Greece; and it was not till some two generations after the Conquest, that learning and literature regained in England somewhat of the position which they had occupied two centuries earlier. And this new literary culture was naturally confined to the French dialect of the conquerors, which had become the language of court and castle, of church and law, of chivalry and the chase; while the rich and cultured tongue of Alfred and Ælfric was left for generations without literary employment, during which time it lost nearly all its poetical, philosophical, scientific, and artistic vocabulary, retaining only the words of common life and everyday use [4] . And for more than 300 years after the Conquest English lexicography stood still. Between 1066 and 1400, Wright-Wülcker shows only two meagre vocabularies, occupying some twenty-four columns of his volume. One of these, of the twelfth century, is only an echo of the earlier literary age, a copy of a pre-Conquest glossary, which some scribe who could still read the classical tongue of the old West Saxon Court, transliterated into the corrupted forms of his own generation. The other is a short vocabulary of the Latin and vernacular names of plants, a species of class-vocabulary of which there exist several of rather early date.

But when we reach the end of the fourteenth century, English is once more in the ascendant. Robert of Gloucester, Robert Mannyng of Brunne, Dan Michel of Canterbury, and Richard Rolle of Hampole, William Langland and John Wyclif, John Gower and Geoffrey Chaucer, and many other authors of less known or entirely unknown name, have written in the tongue of the people; English has been sanctioned for use in the courts of law; and, as John of Trevisa tells us, has, since the 'furste moreyn' or Great Pestilence of 1349 (which Mrs. Markham has taught nineteenth-century historians to call the 'Black Death'), been introduced into the grammar schools in the translation of Latin exercises, which boys formerly rendered into French. And under these new conditions lexicographical activity at once bursts forth with vigour. Six important vocabularies of the fifteenth century are printed by Wright-Wülcker, most of them arranged, like the Old English one of Ælfric, under subject-headings; but one large one, extending to 2,500 words, entirely alphabetical. About the middle of the century, also, was compiled the famous *Medulla Grammatices* [5], designated, with some propriety, 'the first Latin-English Dictionary,' the popularity of which is shown by the many manuscript copies that still survive; while it formed the basis of the *Ortus* (i.e. *Hortus*) *Vocabulorum* or first printed Latin-English Dictionary, which issued from the press of Wynkyn de Worde in 1500, and in many subsequent editions down to 1533, as well as in an edition by Pynson in 1509.

But all the glossaries and vocabularies as yet mentioned were Latin-English; their primary object was not English, but the elucidation of Latin. A momentous advance was made about 1440, when Brother Galfridus Grammaticus—Geoffrey the Grammarian—a Dominican friar of Lynn Episcopi in Norfolk, produced the English-Latin vocabulary, to which he gave the name of *Promptuarium* or *Promptorium Parvulorum*, the Children's Store-room or Repository.

The *Promptorium*, the name of which has now become a household word to students of the history of English, is a vocabulary containing some 10,000 words—substantives, adjectives, and verbs—with their Latin equivalents, which, as edited by Mr. Albert Way for the Camden Society in 1865, makes a goodly volume. Many manuscript copies of it were made and circulated, of which six or seven are known to be still in existence, and after the introduction of printing it passed through many editions in the presses of Pynson, Wynkyn de Worde, and Julian Notary.

Later in the same century, the year 1483 saw the compilation of a similar, but quite independent work, which its author named the *Catholicon Anglicum*, that is, the English Catholicon or Universal treatise, after the name of the celebrated Latin dictionary of the Middle Ages, the *Catholicon* or *Summa* of Johannes de Balbis, or John of Genoa, made in 1286. The English *Catholicon* was in itself a work almost equally valuable with the *Promptorium*; but it appears never to have attained to the currency of the *Promptorium*, which appeared as a printed book in 1499, while the *Catholicon* remained in two MSS. till printed for the Early English Text Society in 1881.

The Renascence of Ancient Learning had now reached England, and during the sixteenth century there were compiled and published many important Latin-English and English-Latin vocabularies and dictionaries. Among these special mention must be made of the Dictionary of Sir Thomas Elyot, Knight, the first work, so far as I know, which took to itself in English what was destined to be the famous name of DICTIONARY, in mediaeval Latin, *Dictionarius liber*, or *Dictionarium*, literally a repertory of *dictiones*, a word originally meaning 'sayings,' but already by the later Latin grammarians used in the sense of *verba* or *vocabula* 'words.' The early vocabularies and dictionaries had many names, often quaint and striking; thus one of *c*1420 is entitled the *Nominale*, or Name-book; mention has already been made of the *Medulla Grammatices*, or Marrow of Grammar, the *Ortus Vocabulorum*, or Garden of Words, the *Promptorium Parvulorum*, and the *Catholicon Anglicum*; later we find the *Manipulus Vocabulorum*, or Handful of Vocables, the *Alvearie* or Beehive, the *Abecedarium*, the *Bibliotheca*, or Library, the *Thesaurus*, or Treasury of Words—what Old English times would have called the *Word-hord*, the *World of Words*, the *Table Alphabetical*, the *English Expositor*, the *Ductor in Linguas*, or Guide to the Tongues, the *Glossographia*, the *New World of Words*, the *Etymologicum*, the *Gazophylacium*; and it would have been impossible to predict in the year 1538, when Sir Thomas Elyot published his 'Dictionary,' that this name would supplant all the others, and even take the place of the older and better-descended word *Vocabulary*; much less that *Dictionary* should become so much a name to conjure with, as to be applied to works which are not word-books at all, but reference-books on all manner of subjects, as Chronology, Geography, Music, Commerce, Manufactures, Chemistry, or National Biography, arranged in Alphabetical or 'Dictionary order.' The very phrase, 'Dictionary order,' would in the first half of the sixteenth century have been unmeaning, for all dictionaries were not yet alphabetical. There is indeed no other connexion between a dictionary and alphabetical order, than that of a balance of convenience. Experience has shown that though an alphabetical order makes the matter of a dictionary very disjointed, scattering the terminology of a particular art, science, or subject, all over the book, and even when related words come together, often putting the unimportant derivative in front of the important primitive word, it is yet that by which a word or heading can be found, with least trouble and exercise of thought. But this experience has been only gradually acquired; even now the native dictionaries of some Oriental languages are often not in alphabetical order; in such a language as Chinese, indeed, there is no alphabetical order in which to place the words, and they follow each other in the dictionary in a purely arbitrary and conventional fashion. In English, as we have seen, many of the vocabularies from the eleventh to the fifteenth century, were arranged under class-headings according to subject; and, although Sir Thomas Elyot's Dictionary was actually in alphabetical order, that of J. Withals, published in 1554, under the title 'A short dictionarie for young beginners,' and with the colophon 'Thus endeth this Dictionary very useful for Children, compiled by J. Withals,' reverts to the older arrangement of subject-classes, as Names of things in the Æther or skie, the xii Signes, the vii Planets, Tymes, Seasons, Other times in the yere, the daies of the weeke, the Ayre, the viii windes, the iiii partes of the worlde, Byrdes, Bees, Flies, and other, the Water, the Sea, Fishes, a Shippe with other Water vessels, the earth, Mettales, Serpents, woorms and creepinge beastes, Foure-footed beastes, &c. [6]

It is unnecessary in this lecture to recount even the names of the Latin-English and English-Latin dictionaries of the sixteenth century. It need only be mentioned that there were six successive and successively enlarged editions of Sir Thomas Elyot; that the last three of these were edited by Thomas Cooper, 'Schole-Maister of Maudlens in Oxford' (the son of an Oxford tradesman, and educated as a chorister in Magdalen College School, who rose to be Dean of Christ Church and Vice-Chancellor of the University, and to hold successively the episcopal sees of Lincoln and Winchester), and that Cooper, in 1565, published his great *Thesaurus Linguæ Romanæ et Britannicæ*, 'opera et industria Thomæ Cooperi Magdalenensis,' founded upon the great French work of Robert Stephens (Estienne), the learned French scholar and printer. Of this work Martin Marprelate says in his *Epistle* (Arber, p. 42), 'His Lordship of Winchester is a great Clarke, for he hath translated his Dictionarie, called Cooper's Dictionarie, verbatim out of Robert Stephanus his *Thesaurus*, and ill-favoured too, they say!' This was, however, the criticism of an adversary; Cooper had added to Stephens's work many accessions from his editions of Sir Thomas Elyot, and other sources; his *Thesaurus* was the basis of later Latin-English dictionaries, and traces of it may still be discovered in the Latin-English dictionaries of to-day.

Of printed English-Latin works, after the *Promptorium*, one of the earliest was the *Vulgaria* of William Herman, Headmaster and Provost of Eton, printed by Pynson in 1519. This is a *Dictionarium* or *liber dictionarius* in the older sense, for it consists of short *dictiones* or sayings, maxims, and remarks, arranged under subject-headings, such as *De Pietate*, *De Impietate*, *De corporis dotibus*, *De Valetudinis cura*, *De Hortensibus*, *De Bellicis*, and finally a heading *Promiscua*. It may therefore be conceived that it is not easy to find any particular *dictio*. Horman was originally a Cambridge man; but, according to Wood, he was elected a Fellow of New College, Oxford, in 1477, the very year in which Caxton printed his first book in England, and in this connexion it is interesting to find among the illustrative sentences in the *Vulgaria*, this reference to the new art (sign. Oij): 'The prynters haue founde a crafte to make bokes by brasen letters sette in ordre by a frame,' which is thus latinized: 'Chalcographi artem excogitauerunt imprimendi libros qua literæ formis æreis excudunt.' Of later English-Latin dictionaries two deserve passing mention: the *Abecedarium* of Richard Huloet or Howlet, a native of Wisbech, which appeared in the reign of Edward VI, in 1552, and the Alvearie of John Baret, Fellow of Trinity College, Cambridge, published under Elizabeth in 1573. The Abecedarium, although it gives the Latin equivalents, may be looked upon to some extent as an English dictionary, for many of the words have an English explanation, as well as a Latin rendering; thus *Almesse*, or gift of dryncke, meate, or money, distributed to the poore, *sporta, sportula*; *Amyable*, pleasante, or hauing a good grace, *amabilis*; *Anabaptistes*, a sorte of heretyques of late tyme in Germanye about the yere of our Lorde God 1524.... *Anabaptistæ*.

Baret's *Alvearie* of 1573 has been justly styled 'one of the most quaint and charming of all the early Dictionaries.' In his 'Prefatory Address to the Reader' the author tells, in fine Elizabethan prose, both how his book came into existence, and why he gave it its curious name:—

> About eighteene yeeres agone, hauing pupils at Cambridge studious of the Latine tongue, I vsed them often to write Epistles and Theames together, and dailie to translate some peece of English into Latine, for the more speedie attaining of the same. And after we had a little begun, perceiuing

what great trouble it was to come running to me for euerie worde they missed, knowing then of no other Dictionarie to helpe vs, but Sir Thomas Eliots Librarie, which was come out a little before; I appointed them certaine leaues of the same booke euerie daie to write the english before the Latin, & likewise to gather a number of fine phrases out of Cicero, Terence, Cæsar, Liuie, &c. & to set them vnder seuerall titles, for the more readie finding them againe at their neede. Thus, within a yeere or two, they had gathered together a great volume, which (for the apt similitude betweene the good Scholers and diligent Bees in gathering their waxe and honie into their Hiue) I called then their *Aluearie*, both for a memoriall by whom it was made, and also by this name to incourage other to the like diligence, for that they should not see their worthie praise for the same, vnworthilie drowned in obliuion. Not long after, diuers of our friends borrowing this our worke which we had thus contriued & wrought onelie for our owne priuate vse, often and many waies moued me to put it in print for the common profet of others, and the publike propagation of the Latine tongue.

But when Baret at length resolved to comply with this suggestion, there were many difficulties to be overcome, the expense of the work being not the least:—

And surelie, had not the right honourable Sir Thomas Smith knight, principall Secretarie to the Queenes Maiestie, that noble Theseus of learning, and comfortable Patrone to all Students, and the right Worshipfull M. Nowell, Deane of Pawles, manie waies encouraged me in this wearie worke (the charges were so great, and the losse of my time so much grieued me) I had neuer bene able alone to haue wrestled against so manie troubles, but long ere this had cleane broken off our worke begun, and cast it by for euer.

Between the dates of the *Abecedarium* and the *Alvearie*, Peter Levins, Fellow of Magdalen College, Oxford, published, in 1570, the first essay at an English Riming Dictionary, the *Manipulus Vocabulorum*, or Handful of Vocables, an original copy of which is in the Bodleian Library; it was reprinted for the Early English Text Society in 1867 by Mr. H. B. Wheatley. The English words are arranged in order of their terminations, and each is furnished with a Latin equivalent.

Of all the works which we have yet considered, Latin was an essential element: whether the object was, as in the glossaries and vocabularies before the fifteenth century, to explain the Latin words themselves, or as in the *Promptorium* and *Catholicon*, the *Abecedarium* and the *Alvearie*, and other works of the sixteenth century, to render English words into Latin. But a new stage of development was marked by the appearance of dictionaries of English with another modern language. In 1521, the 'Introductory to write and to pronounce Frenche,' by Alexander Barclay, author of the 'Ship of Fooles,' was issued from the press of Robert Coplande; and about 1527 Giles du Guez or du Wes (anglicized Dewes), French teacher to the Lady Mary, afterwards Queen Mary, published his 'Introductorie for to lerne to rede, to pronounce and to speke French trewly.' In addition to grammatical rules and dialogues, it contains a select vocabulary English and French. In 1514, Mary Tudor, younger sister of Henry VIII, became the unwilling bride of Louis XII of France. To initiate the princess in her husband's tongue, John Palsgrave, a native of London and graduate of Cambridge, who had subsequently studied in Paris, was chosen as her tutor, and accompanied her to France. For her use Palsgrave prepared his celebrated *Esclarcissement de la Langue Françoyse*, which he subsequently revised and published in 1530, after his return to England, where he was incorporated M.A. at Oxford. The *Esclarcissement* is a famous book, at once grammar and vocabulary, and may be considered as the earliest dictionary of a modern language, in French as well as in English. It was reprinted in 1852 at the expense of the French Government in the series of publications entitled 'Collection de documents inédits sur l'histoire de France, publiés par les soins du Ministre de l'Instruction Publique, Deuxième Série—Histoire des Lettres et des Sciences.' It is a trite saying that 'they do these things better in France'; but it is, nevertheless, sometimes true. Amid all the changes of government which France has seen in modern times, it has never been forgotten that the history of the French language, and of French letters and French science, is part of the history of France; the British government has not even now attained to the standpoint of recognizing this: among the historical documents published under the direction of the authorities of the Record Office, there is no series illustrating the history of the language, the literature, or the science of England.

Next to French, the continental languages most important to Englishmen in the sixteenth century, were Italian and Spanish, of both of which, accordingly, dictionaries were published before the end of the century[7]. In 1599 Richard Percevall, Gent., published his dictionary in Spanish and English; and in the same year 'resolute John Florio' (who in his youth resided in Worcester Place, Oxford, and was matriculated at Magdalen College in

1581) brought out his Italian-English Dictionary, the *World of Words*, which he re-published in a much enlarged form in 1611, with dedication to the Queen of James I, as *Queen Anna's New World of Words*. This year, also, Randall Cotgrave published his famous French-English Dictionary, which afterwards passed through so many editions. In the absence as yet of any merely English dictionary, the racy English vocabulary of Florio and Cotgrave is of exceeding value, and has been successfully employed in illustrating the contemporary language of Shakspere, to whom Florio, patronized as he was by the Earls of Southampton and Pembroke, was probably personally known. Thus, the same year which saw England provided with the version of the Bible which was to be so intimately identified with the language of the next three centuries, saw her also furnished with adequate dictionaries of French, Italian, and Spanish; and, in 1617, a still more ambitious work was accomplished by John Minsheu in the production of a polyglot dictionary of English with ten other languages, British or Welsh, Low Dutch, High Dutch, French, Italian, Spanish, Portuguese, Latin, Greek, and Hebrew, which he entitled 'Ηγεμων εις τας γλωσσας, id est *Ductor in Linguas*, the Guide into Tongues.'

But though in these works there is necessarily contained much of the material of an English dictionary, so that we can from them recover most of the current vocabulary, no one appears before the end of the sixteenth century to have felt that Englishmen could want a dictionary to help them to the knowledge and correct use of their own language. That language was either an in-born faculty, or it was inhaled with their native air, or imbibed with their mothers' milk; how could they need a book to teach them to speak their mother-tongue? To the scholars of the Renascence the notion would have seemed absurd—as absurd as it has seemed to some of their descendants in the nineteenth century, that an English grammar-school or an English university should trouble itself about such aboriginal products of the English skull, as English language and literature. But by the end of the sixteenth century, as by the end of the nineteenth, there was a moving of the waters: the Renascence of ancient learning had itself brought into English use thousands of learned words, from Latin, Greek, Hebrew, Arabic, and other languages, 'ink-horn terms,' as they were called by Bale and by Puttenham, unknown to, and not to be imbibed from, mother or grandmother. A work exhibiting the spelling, and explaining the meaning, of these new-fangle 'hard words' was the felt want of the day; and the first attempt to supply it marks, on the whole, the most important point in the evolution of the modern English Dictionary.

In 1604, Robert Cawdrey, who had been a schoolmaster at Okeham, and afterwards at Coventry, published a modest octavo of 120 pages, 5½ inches by 3½, calling itself *The Table Alphabeticall of Hard Words*, in which he set forth the proper spelling and meaning of some 3,000 of these learned terms; his work reached a third edition in 1612 [8] . In 1616, Dr. John Bullokar, then resident in Chichester, followed with a work of the same kind and size, named by him *An English Expositor*, of which numerous editions came out, one as late as 1684. And in 1623 appeared the work which first assumed the title of 'The English Dictionarie,' by H.C., Gent. H.C., we learn from the dedication, was Henry Cockeram, to whom John Ford the dramatist addressed the following congratulatory lines:—

To my industrious friend, the Author of this English Dictionarie,
MR. HENRY COCKRAM OF EXETER.

Borne in the West? liue there? so far from Court?

From Oxford, Cambridge, London? yet report

(Now in these daies of Eloquence) such change

Of words? vnknown? vntaught? tis new and strange.

Let Gallants therefore skip no more from hence

To Italic, France, Spaine, and with expence

Waste time and faire estates, to learne new fashions

Of complementall phrases, soft temptations

To glorious beggary: Here let them hand

This Booke; here studie, reade, and vnderstand:

Then shall they find varietie at Home,

As curious as at Paris, or at Rome.

For my part I confesse, hadst not thou writ,

I had not beene acquainted with more wit

Than our old English taught; but now I can

Be proud to know I have a Countryman

Hath strugled for a fame, and what is more,

Gain'd it by paths of Art, vntrod before.

The benefit is generall; the crowne

Of praise particular, and thats *thine owne.*

What should I say? thine owne deserts inspire thee,

Twere base to enuie, I must then admire thee.

A friend and louer of thy paines,
IOHN FORD.

And a deeply interesting little book is this diminutive ancestor of the modern English Dictionary, to describe which adequately would take far more time than the limits of this lecture afford. It is divided into three parts: Part I contains the hard words with their explanation in ordinary language; and instructive it is to see what words were then considered hard and unknown. Many of them certainly would be so still: as, for example, *abgregate*, 'to lead out of the flock'; *acersecomick*, 'one whose hair was never cut'; *adcorporated*, 'married'; *adecastick*, 'one that will do just howsoever'; *bubulcitate*, 'to cry like a cow-boy'; *collocuplicate*, 'to enrich'—concerning which we wonder who used them, or where Cockeram found them; but we are surprised to find among these hard words *abandon*, *abhorre*, *abrupt*, *absurd*, *action*, *activitie*, and *actresse*, explained as 'a woman doer,' for the stage actress had not yet appeared. *Blunder*, 'to bestir oneself,' and *Garble*, 'to clense things from dust,' remind us that the meanings of words are subject to change. The Second Part contains the ordinary words 'explained' by their hard equivalents, and is intended to teach a learned style. The plain man or gentlewoman may write a letter in his or her natural language, and then by turning up the simple words in the dictionary alter them into their learned equivalents. Thus 'abound' may be altered into *exuperate*, 'too great plenty' into *uberty*, 'he and I are of one age' into *we are coetaneous*, 'youthful babbling' into *juvenile inaniloquence*—a useful expression to hurl at an opponent in the Oxford Union.

The last part is the most entertaining of all: it is headed 'The Third Part, treating of Gods and Goddesses, Men and Women, Boyes and Maides, Giants and Diuels, Birds and Beasts, Monsters and Serpents, Wells and Riuers, Herbes, Stones, Trees, Dogges, Fishes, and the like'; it is a key to the allusions to classical, historical, mythological, and other marvellous persons, animals, and things, to be met with in polite literature. A good example of its contents is the well-known article on the *Crocodile*:—

> *Crocodile*, a beast hatched of an egge, yet some of them grow
> to a great bignesse, as 10. 20. or 30. foot in length: it hath
> cruell teeth and scaly back, with very sharpe clawes on his
> feete: if it see a man afraid of him, it will eagerly pursue
> him, but on the contrary, if he be assaulted he wil shun him.
> Hauing eaten the body of a man, it will weepe ouer the head,
> but in fine eate the head also: thence came the Prouerb, he
> shed Crocodile teares, viz., fayned teares.

Appreciation of Cockeram's 'Dictionarie' was marked by the numerous editions through which it passed down as late as 1659. Meanwhile Thomas Blount, Barrister of the Inner Temple, and correspondent of Anthony à Wood, was devoting the leisure hours of twenty years to his '*Glossographia*:

or a Dictionary interpreting all such hard words, whether Hebrew, Greek, Latin,' etc., 'as are now used in our refined English Tongue,' of which the first edition saw the light in 1656.

I suppose it is a truism, that the higher position now taken by English studies, is intimately interwoven with the advances which have been made during the last quarter of a century in the higher education of women, and that but for the movement to let women share in the advantages of a university education, it is doubtful whether the nineteenth century would have witnessed the establishment of a School of English Language and Literature at Oxford. In connexion with this it is a noteworthy fact, that the preparation of these early seventeenth century English dictionaries was also largely due to a consideration of the educational wants of women. The 'Table Alphabeticall' of Robert Cawdrey, which was dedicated to five 'right honourable, Worshipfull, vertuous, and godlie Ladies[9],' the sisters of his former pupil, Sir James Harrington, Knight, bears on its title-page that it is 'gathered for the benefit and help of Ladies, Gentlewomen, or any other vnskilfull persons.' Bullokar's *Expositor* was dedicated 'to the Right Honorable and Vertvovs his Singvlar Good Ladie, the Ladie Jane Viscountesse Mountague,' under whose patronage he hoped to see the work 'perhaps gracefully admitted among greatest Ladies and studious Gentlewomen, to whose reading (I am made belieue) it will not prooue altogether vngratefull.' In similar words, the title-page of Cockeram's Dictionary proclaims its purpose of 'Enabling as well Ladies and Gentlewomen ... as also Strangers of any Nation to the vnderstanding of the more difficult Authors already printed in our Language, and the more speedy attaining of an elegant perfection of the English tongue, both in reading, speaking, and writing.' And Thomas Blount, setting forth the purpose of his *Glossographia*, says, in words of which one seems to have heard an echo in reference to an English School in this University, 'It is chiefly intended for the more-knowing Women, and less-knowing Men; or indeed for all such of the unlearned, who can but finde in an Alphabet the word they understand not.'

It is noticeable that all these references to the needs of women disappear from the later editions, and are wanting in later dictionaries after 1660; whether this was owing to the fact that the less-knowing women had now come upsides with the more-knowing men; or that with the Restoration, female education went out of fashion, and women sank back again into elegant illiteracy, I leave to the historian to discover; I only, as a lexicographer, record the fact that from the Restoration the dictionaries are silent about the education of women, till we pass the Revolution settlement and reach the Age of Queen Anne, when J.K. in 1702 tells us that his dictionary is 'chiefly designed for the benefit of young Scholars, Tradesmen, Artificers, and the female sex, who would learn to spell truely.'

Blount's *Glossographia* went through many editions down to 1707; but two years after its appearance, Edward Phillips, the son of Milton's sister Anne, published his *New World of Words*, which Blount with some reason considered to be largely plagiarized from his book. He held his peace, however, until Phillips brought out a Law-Dictionary or *Nomothetes*, also largely copied from his own *Nomo-lexicon*, when he could refrain himself no longer, and burst upon the world with his indignant pamphlet, 'A World of Errors discovered in the New World of Words, and in Nomothetes or the Interpreter,' in which he exhibits the proofs of Phillips's cribbing, and makes wild sport of the cases in which his own errors and misprints had either been copied or muddled by his plagiarist. The latter did not vouchsafe a reply; he knew a better plan; he quietly corrected in his next edition the mistakes which Blount had so conveniently pointed out, and his 'New World of Words,' furnished with an engraved frontispiece, containing views of Oxford and Cambridge, and portraits of some Oxford and Cambridge scholars, lived on in successive editions as long as Blount's.

Time and space forbid me even to recount the later dictionaries of this class and period; we need only mention that of Elisha Coles, a chorister and subsequently matriculated student of Magdalen College (of which his uncle, Elisha Coles, was steward under the Commonwealth), a meritorious work which passed through numerous editions down to 1732; and that of Edward Cocker, the celebrated arithmetician and writing-master of St. George's, Southwark, by whom people still sometimes asseverate 'according to Cocker.' This was published after his death, 'from the author's correct copy,' by John Hawkins, in 1704, with a portrait of the redoubtable Cocker himself in flowing wig and gown, and the following lines:—

> COCKER, who in fair writing did excell,
>
> And in Arithmetic perform'd as well,
>
> This necessary work took next in hand,
>
> That Englishmen might English understand.

The last edition of Phillips' *New World of Words* was edited after his death, with numerous additions, by John Kersey, son of John Kersey the mathematician. Two years later Kersey threw the materials into another form and published it in an octavo, as Kersey's '*Dictionarium Anglo-Britannicum*, or a General English Dictionary,' of which three editions appeared before 1721. In this work there are included a considerable number of obsolete words, chiefly from Spenser and his contemporaries, marked O., and in some cases erroneously explained. Professor Skeat has pointed out that this was the source of Chatterton's Elizabethan vocabulary, and that he took the obsolete words, which he attributed to Rowley, erroneous explanations and all, direct from Kersey's Dictionary.

More than 100 years had now elapsed since Robert Cawdrey prepared his 'Table Alphabeticall,' and nearly a century since the work of Cockeram; and all the dictionaries which had meanwhile appeared, although their size had steadily increased, were, in purpose and fact, only what these works had been—Vocabularies of 'Hard Words,' not of words in general. The notion that an English Dictionary ought to contain *all* English words had apparently as yet occurred to no one; at least no one had proposed to carry the idea into practice. But this further step in the evolution of the modern dictionary was now about to be made, and the man who made it was one of the most deserving in the annals of English lexicography. We now, looking back on the eighteenth century, associate it chiefly with the work of Dr. Johnson; but down beyond the middle of that century, and to the man in the street much later, by far the best-known name in connexion with dictionaries was that of NATHANAEL BAILEY. An advertisement appended to the first edition of his Dictionary runs thus: 'Youth Boarded, and taught the Hebrew, Greek, and Latin languages, in a Method more Easy and Expedient than is common; also, other School-learning, by the *Author* of this *Dictionary*, to be heard of at Mr. Batley's, Bookseller, at the Sign of the Dove in Paternoster Row.' Bailey was the author or editor of several scholarly works; but, for us, his great work was his *Universal Etymological English Dictionary*, published in 1721. In this he aimed at including all English words; yet not for the mere boast of 'completeness,' but for a practical purpose. The dictionary was not merely explanatory, it was also etymological; and though Englishmen might not need to be told the meaning of *man* or *woman*, *dog* or *cat* [10], they might want a hint as to their derivation. Bailey had hit the nail aright: successive editions were called for almost every two years during the century; when the author died, in 1742, the tenth edition was in the press. In that of 1731, Bailey first marked the stress-accent, a step in the direction of indicating pronunciation. In 1730, moreover, he brought out with the aid of some specialists, his folio dictionary, the greatest lexicographical work yet undertaken in English, into which he also introduced diagrams and proverbs. This is an interesting book historically, for, according to Sir John Hawkins, it formed the working basis of Dr. Johnson[11].

Bailey had many imitators and rivals, nearly all of whom aimed, like him, at including all words; of these I need only name Dyche and Pardon 1735, B.N. Defoe 1735, and Benjamin Martin 1749.

During the second quarter of the century, the feeling arose among literary men, as well as among the booksellers, that the time had come for the preparation of a 'Standard Dictionary' of the English tongue. The language had now attained a high degree of literary perfection; a perfect prose style, always a characteristic of maturity, had been created; a brilliant galaxy of dramatists and essayists—Dryden, Pope, Addison, Steele, Swift, Defoe—had demonstrated that English was capable of expressing clearly and elegantly everything that needed to be expressed in language. The age of Queen Anne was compared to the Ciceronian age of Latin, or the age of Aristotle and Plato in Greek. But in both these cases, as indeed in that of every known ancient people, the language, after reaching its acme of perfection, had begun to decay and become debased: the golden age of Latinity had passed into a silvern, and that into a brazen and an iron age. The fear was that a like fate should overtake English also; to avert which calamity the only remedy appeared to be to *fix the language* by means of a 'Standard Dictionary,' which should register the proper sense and use of every word and phrase, from which no polite writer henceforth would be expected to deviate; but, even as generation after generation of boys and men found their perfection of Latinity in the imitation of Cicero, so all succeeding ages of Englishmen should find their ideal of speech and writing fixed for ever in this standard dictionary. To us of a later age, with our fuller knowledge of the history of language, and our wider experience of its fortunes, when it has to be applied to entirely new fields of knowledge, such as have been opened to us since the birth of modern science, this notion seems childlike and pathetic. But it was eminently characteristic of the eighteenth century, an age of staid and decorous subsidence from the energetic restlessness of the seventeenth—an age in which men eschewed revolution and innovation, and devoted themselves assiduously to conserve, consolidate, polish, refine, and make the best of what they had.

In this notion of ascertaining, purifying, refining, and fixing the language, England was only following in the wake of some other countries. In Italy the *Accademia della Crusca*, and in France the *Academie française*, had been instituted for this very purpose, and the latter had, after twenty years of preparation, and forty more years of work, published the first edition of a dictionary in which the French language was (fondly and vainly) supposed to be thus ascertained, sifted, and fixed for ever. England had no Academy; but it was thought that what had been done in France by the Forty Immortals might perhaps be done here by some leading man of letters. The idea had, it appears, been put before Alexander Pope, and approved by him; he is said even to have drawn up a list of the authors whose writings might be taken as authorities for such a dictionary; but he died in 1744, before anything further was done. The subject seems then to have been pressed upon the attention of SAMUEL JOHNSON; but it was not till 1747 that the matter took definite shape, when a syndicate of five or six London booksellers contracted with Johnson to produce the desired standard dictionary in the space of three years for the sum of fifteen hundred guineas. Alas for human calculations, and especially for those of dictionary makers! The work occupied nearly thrice the specified time, and, ere it was finished, the stipulated sum had been considerably overdrawn. At length, in 1755, appeared the two massive folios, each 17 inches long, 10 inches wide, and 3½ inches thick, entitled 'A | Dictionary | of the | English Language | in which | the Words are deduced from their Originals, | and | illustrated in their different significations | by Examples from the Best Writers. | By Samuel Johnson.' The limits of this lecture do not permit me to say one tithe of what might and ought to be said of this great work. For the present purpose it must suffice to point out that the special new feature which it contributed to the evolution of the modern dictionary was the illustration of the use of each word by a selection of literary quotations, and the more delicate appreciation and discrimination of senses which this involved and rendered possible. Only where he had no quotations did Johnson insert words from Bailey's folio, or other source, with *Dict.* as the authority. The literary quotations were entirely supplied by himself from his capacious memory, or from books specially perused and marked by him for extraction. When he first began his work in the room in Gough Square, his whole time was devoted to thus reading and marking books, from which six clerkly assistants copied the marked quotations. The fact that many of the quotations were inserted from memory without verification (a practice facilitated by Johnson's plan of merely naming the author, without specifying the particular work quoted, or giving any reference whereby the passage could be turned up) is undoubtedly the reason why many of the quotations are not verbally exact. Even so, however, they are generally adequate for the purpose for which they are adduced, that is, they usually contain the word for which they are quoted, and the context is more or less accurately rendered. But in some cases it is otherwise: Johnson's memory played him false, and he quotes a passage for a word that it does not actually contain. As an example, under *Distilment* he correctly quotes from *Hamlet*, 'And in the porches of mine ears did pour the leperous distilment.' But when he reached *Instilment*, his memory became vague, and forgetting that he had already quoted the passage under *Distilment*, he quoted it again as 'the leperous instilment'—a reading which does not exist in any text of Shakspere, and was a mere temporary hallucination of memory. There are some other curious mistakes, which must, I suppose, have crept in either in the course of transcription or of printing. As specimens I mention two, because they have unfortunately perverted ordinary usage. The two words *Coco* and *Cocoa*—the former a Portuguese word [12] , naming the *coco-nut*, the fruit of a palm-tree; the latter a latinized form of *Cacao*, the Aztec name of a Central American shrub, whence we have cocoa and chocolate—were always distinguished down to Johnson's time, and were in fact distinguished by Johnson himself in his own writings. His account of these in the Dictionary is quoted from Miller's *Gardener's Dictionary* and Hill's *Materia Medica*, in which the former is spelt *coco* and the latter *cacao* and *cocoa*. But in Johnson's Dictionary the two words are by some accident run together under the heading *cocoa*, with the disastrous result that modern vulgar usage mixes the two up, spells the *coco-nut*, 'cocoa-' as if it were *co-cō-a*, and on the other hand pronounces *cocōa*, the cacāo-bean and the beverage, as if it were *coco*. The word *dispatch*, from It. *dispaccio*, had been in English use for some 250 years when Johnson's Dictionary appeared, and had been correctly spelt by everybody (that is by everybody but the illiterate) with *dis-*. This was Johnson's own spelling both before and after he published the dictionary, as may be seen in his *Letters* edited by Dr. G. Birkbeck Hill[13]. It was also the spelling of all the writers whom Johnson quoted. But by some inexplicable error, the word got into the dictionary as *despatch*, and this spelling was even substituted in most of the quotations. I have not found that a single writer followed this erroneous spelling in the eighteenth century: Nelson, Wellesley, Wellington, and all our commanders and diplomatists wrote *Dispatches*; but since about 1820, the filtering down of the influence of Johnson's Dictionary has caused this erroneous spelling *despatch* to become generally known and to be looked upon as authoritative; so that at the present time about half our newspapers give the erroneous form, to which, more larmentably, the Post Office, after long retaining the correct official tradition, recently capitulated.

But despite small blemishes[14], the dictionary was a marvellous piece of work to accomplish in eight and a half years; and it is quite certain that, if all the quotations had had to be verified and furnished with exact references, a much longer time, or the employment of much more collaboration, would have been required. With much antecedent preparation, with much skilled co-operation, and with strenuous effort, it took more than nine years to produce the first three letters of the alphabet of the Oxford New English Dictionary.

Johnson's great work raised English lexicography altogether to a higher level. In his hands it became a department of literature. The value of the Dictionary was recognized from the first by men of letters; a second edition was called for the same year. But it hardly became a popular work, or even a work of popular fame, before the present century. For forty years after its first publication editions of Bailey followed each other as rapidly as ever;

numerous new dictionaries of the size and character of Bailey, often largely indebted to Johnson's definitions, appeared. But the only new feature introduced into lexicography between 1755 and the end of the century was the indication of the Orthoepy or Pronunciation. From Bailey onward, and by Johnson himself, the place of the stress-accent had been marked, but no attempt had been made to show how such a group of letters, for example, as *colonel*, or *enough*, or *phthisical*, was actually pronounced; or, to use modern phraseology, to tell what the *living word* itself was, as distinguished from its written symbol. This feature, so obviously important in a language of which the spelling had ceased to be phonetic, was added by Dr. William Kenrick in his 'New Dictionary' of 1773, a little later in 1775 by William Perry, in 1780 by Thomas Sheridan, and especially in 1791 by John Walker, whose authority long remained as supreme in the domain of pronunciation, as that of Dr. Johnson in definition and illustration; so that popular dictionaries of the first half of the present century commonly claimed to be abridgements of 'Johnson's Dictionary, with, the Pronunciation on the basis of Walker.'

From the first quarter of the nineteenth century, the lexicographical supremacy of Johnson's Dictionary was undisputed, and eminent students of the language busied themselves in trying, not to supersede it, but to supplement and perfect it. Numerous supplements, containing additional words, senses, and quotations, were published; in 1818 a new edition, embracing many such accessions, was prepared by the learned Archdeacon Todd, and 'Todd's Johnson' continues to be an esteemed work to our own day. But only two independent contributions to the development of lexicography were made in the earlier half of the nineteenth century. These were the American work of Noah Webster, and the English work of Dr. Charles Richardson.

Webster was a great man, a born definer of words; he was fired with the idea that America ought to have a dictionary of its own form of English, independent of British usage, and he produced a work of great originality and value. Unfortunately, like many other clever men, he had the notion that derivations can be elaborated from one's own consciousness as well as definitions, and he included in his work so-called 'etymologies' of this sort. But Etymology is simply Word-history, and Word-history, like all other history, is a record of the *facts* which *did* happen, not a fabric of conjectures as to what may have happened. In the later editions of Webster, these 'derivations' have been cleared out *en masse*, and the etymology placed in the hands of men abreast of the science of the time; and the last edition of Webster, the *International*, is perhaps the best of one-volume dictionaries.

Richardson started on a new track altogether. Observing how much light was shed on the meaning of words by Johnson's quotations, he was impressed with the notion that, in a dictionary, definitions are unnecessary, that quotations alone are sufficient; and he proceeded to carry this into effect by making a dictionary without definitions or explanations of meaning, or at least with the merest rudiments of them, but illustrating each group of words by a large series of quotations. In the collection of these he displayed immense research. Going far beyond the limits of Dr. Johnson, he quoted from authors back to the year 1300, and probably for the first time made Chaucer and Gower and Piers Ploughman living names to many readers. And his special notion was quite correct *in theory*. Quotations *will* tell the full meaning of a word, *if one has enough of them*; but it takes a great many to be enough, and it takes a reader a long time to read and weigh all the quotations, and to deduce from them the meanings which might be put before him in a line or two. As a fact, while Richardson's notion was correct in theory, mundane conditions of space and time rendered it humanly impracticable. Nevertheless, the mass of quotations, most of them with exact references, collected by him, and printed under the word-groups which they illustrated, was a service never to be undervalued or forgotten, and his work, 'A New Dictionary of the English Language ... Illustrated by Quotations from the best Authors' by Charles Richardson, LL.D., 1836–7, still continues to be a valuable repertory of illustrations.

Such was the position of English lexicography in the middle of the nineteenth century, when the late Dr. Trench, then Dean of Westminster, who had already written several esteemed works on the English language and the history of words, read two papers before the Philological Society in London 'On some Deficiencies in existing English Dictionaries,' in which, while speaking with much appreciation of the labours of Dr. Johnson and his successors, he declared that these labours yet fell far short of giving us the ideal English Dictionary. Especially, he pointed out that for the *history* of words and families of words, and for the changes of form and sense which words had historically passed through, they gave hardly any help whatever. No one could find out from all the dictionaries extant how long any particular word had been in the language, which of the many senses in which many words were used was the original, or how or when these many senses had been developed; nor, in the case of words described as *obsolete*, were we told *when* they became obsolete or by whom they were last used. He pointed out also that the obsolete and the rarer words of the language had never been completely collected; that thousands of words current in the literature of the past three centuries had escaped the diligence of Johnson and all his supplementers; that, indeed, the collection of the requisite material for a complete dictionary could not be compassed by any one man, however long-lived and however diligent, but must be the work be a biography of every word, and should set forth every fact connected with its origin, history, and use, on a strictly historical method. These stages coincide necessarily with stages of our national and literary history; the first two were already reached before the Norman Conquest; the third followed upon the recognition of English as the official language of the nation, and its employment by illustrious Middle English writers. The Dictionaries of the modern languages were necessitated first by the fact that French had at length ceased to be the living tongue of any class of Englishmen, and secondly by the other fact that the rise of the modern languages and increasing intercourse with the Continent made Latin no longer sufficient as a common medium of international communication. The consequences of the Renascence and of the New Learning of the sixteenth century appear in the need for the Dictionaries of Hard Words at the beginning of the seventeenth; the literary polish of the age of Anne begat the yearning for a standard dictionary, and inspired the work of Johnson; the scientific and historical spirit of the nineteenth century has at once called for and rendered possible the Oxford English Dictionary. Thus the evolution of English Lexicography has followed with no faltering steps the evolution of English History and the development of English Literature.

FOOTNOTES:

[1] Thus the first six Latin words in A glossed are *apodixen, amineæ, amites, arcontus, axungia*; the last six are *arbusta, anser, affricus, atticus, auiaria, avena*; mostly 'hard' Latin it will be perceived. The Erfurt Glossary is, to a great extent, a duplicate of the Epinal.

[2] Thus the first five Latin entries in *ab-* are *abminiculum, abelena, abiecit, absida, abies*, and the last five *aboleri, ab borea, abiles, aborsus, absorduum*. To find whether a wanted word in *ab-* occurs in this glossary, it was necessary to look through more than two columns containing ninety-five entries.

[3] An important collection of these early beginnings of lexicography in England was made so long ago as 1857, by the late distinguished antiquary Thomas Wright, and published as the first volume of a Library of National Antiquities. A new edition of this with sundry emendations and additions was prepared and published in 1884 by Professor R.F. Wülcker of Leipzig, and the collection is now generally referred to by scholars in German fashion under the designation of Wright-Wülcker.

[4] This is the primary reason why in Middle and Modern English, unlike what is found in German and Dutch, the terms of culture, art, science, and philosophy, are of French or, through French, of Latin origin. The corresponding Old English terms were forgotten during the age of illiteracy, and when, generations later, the speaker of English came again to deal with such subjects, he had to do like Layamon, when he knew no longer *tungol-cræft*, and could refer to it only as 'the craft ihote *astronomie* in other kunnes speche.'

[5] Also *Medulla Grammaticae*, or usually *Grammatice*.

[6] At the end is an alphabetical list of adjectives; extending from *lf.* 79*a*, col. 2, to 83*a*, foot.

[7] It must however be mentioned that the second dictionary of English and another modern tongue was appropriately 'A Dictionary in Englyshe and Welshe, moche necessary to all suche Welshemen as wil spedlye learne the englyshe tongue, thought vnto the kynges maiestie very mete to be sette forth to the vse of his graces subiectes in Wales, ... by Wyllyam Salesbury.'

The colophon is 'Imprynted at London in Foster Lane, by me John Waley. 1547.'

[8] In the Dedication he says, 'Which worke, long ago for the most part, was gathered by me, but lately augmented by my sonne Thomas, who now is Schoolemaister in London.'

[9] 'To the right honourable, worshipfull, vertuous, & godlie Ladies, the Lady Hastings, the Lady Dudley, the Lady Mountague, the Ladie Wingfield, and the Lady Leigh, his Christian friends, *R.C.* wisheth great prosperitie in this life, with increase of grace, and peace from GOD our Father, through Iesus Christ our Lord and onely Sauiour.' (A 2.)

[10] His explanations of such words were curt enough: '*Cat*, a Creature well known'; '*Horse*, a Beast well known'; '*Man*, a Creature endued with Reason.'

[11] 'An interleaved copy of Bailey's dictionary in folio he made the repository of the several articles.' *Works of J.*, 1787, I. 175.

[12] Pg. *coco*, a grinning mask, applied to the coco-nut because of the three holes and central protuberance at its apex, suggesting two eyes, a mouth, and nose.

[13] The following are examples of his own practice: *The Rambler* (1751), No. 153, par. 3, 'I was in my eighteenth year dispatched to the university.' *Ibid.*, No. 161, par. 4, 'I ... soon dispatched a bargain on the usual terms.' *Letter to Mrs. Thrale*, May 6, 1776, 'We dispatched our journey very peaceably.'

[14] Among such must be reckoned the treatment of words in the explanation of which Johnson showed political or personal animus or whimsical humour, as in the well-known cases of *whig, tory, excise, pension, pensioner, oats, Grub-street, lexicographer* (see Boswell's *Johnson*, ed. Birkbeck Hill, i. 294); although it must be admitted that these have come to be among the famous spots of the Dictionary, and have given gentle amusement to thousands, to whom it has been a delight to see 'human nature' too strong for lexicographic decorum.

[15] In some cases, long Lists of the Authors, from whose works 'the illustrative quotations have been selected,' are given, without the statement that many of those quotations have not actually been selected from the authors and works named, but have merely been annexed from Johnson or one of his supplementers.

[16] The famous *Deutsches Wörterbuch* of Jacob and Wilhelm Grimm, after many years of preparation, began to be printed in 1852; Jacob Grimm himself died in 1863, in the middle of the letter F; the work is expected to reach the end of S by the close of the century. The great *Woordenboek der Nederlandsche Taal* was commenced in 1852; its first volume, *A–Ajuin*, was published in 1882, and it is not yet quite half-finished. Of the new edition of the *Vocabolario della Crusca*, which is to a certain extent on historical principles, Vol. I, containing A, was published in 1863, and Vol. VIII, completing I, in 1899; at least twenty-five more years will be required to reach Z. None of these works embraces so long a period of the language, or is so strictly historical in method, as the New English Dictionary. Rather are they, like Littré's great *Dictionnaire de la Langue Française*, Dictionaries of the modern language, with the current words more or less historically treated.